# The Yellow House on the Corner

# The
# Yellow House
## on the
# Corner

## poems by
# Rita Dove

*A Carnegie Mellon Classic Contemporary*

Carnegie Mellon University Press
Pittsburgh 1989

*for Fred*

# Acknowledgments:

Some of these poems have appeared in the following magazines and anthologies:

*Antaeus, The American Poetry Anthology, Eating the Menu, Georgia Review, Intro 6, Miami Alumni, Missouri Review, New Honolulu Review, North American Review, Ohio Review, Paris Review, Pearl, Prairie Schooner, Snapdragon, Three Rivers Poetry Journal,* and *The Virginia Quarterly Review.*

"Nigger Song: An Odyssey", "Adolescense—II", and "Planning the Perfect Evening" appeared originally in *Antaeus.* "Robert Schumann, or: Musical Genius Begins with Affliction" and "Small Town" appeared originally in *The Georgia Review.* "Adolescence—III" is reprinted from *Prairie Schooner,* Vol. 49, no. 1 by permission of University of Nebraska Press. Copyright ©1975 by University of Nebraska Press. "The Boast" by Rita Dove from *Intro 6* edited by George Garrett. Copyright ©1974 by Associated Writing Programs. Reprinted by permission of Doubleday & Company, Inc.

The author wishes to thank the National Endowment for the Arts and the Ohio Arts Council for grants which helped support the writing of these poems.

The publication of this book is supported by grants from the National Endowment for the Arts in Washington, D.C., a Federal agency, and from the Pennsylvania Council on the Arts.

Library of Congress Catalog Card Number 80-65700
ISBN 0-88748-092-6
Printed and bound in the United States of America
Second Edition, May 1989

# Contents

I

# This Life

The green lamp flares on the table.
You tell me the same thing
as that one,
asleep, upstairs.
Now I see: the possibilities
are golden dresses in a nutshell.

As a child, I fell in love
with a Japanese woodcut
of a girl gazing at the moon.
I waited with her for her lover.
He came in white breeches and sandals.
He had a goatee—he had

your face, though I didn't know it.
Our lives will be the same—
your lips, swollen from whistling
at danger,
and I a stranger
in this desert,
nursing the tough skins of figs.

# The Bird Frau

When the boys came home, everything stopped
the way he left it—her apron, the back stairs,
the sun losing altitude over France
as the birds scared up from the fields,
a whirring curtain of flak—

                    Barmherzigkeit!
her son, her man. She went inside, fed the parakeet,
broke its neck. Spaetzle bubbling on the stove,
windchimes tinkling above the steam, her face
in the hall mirror, bloated, a heart.
Let everything go wild!

                    Blue jays, crows!
She hung suet from branches, the air quick
around her head with tiny spastic machinery
—starlings, finches—her head a crown of feathers.
She ate less, grew lighter, air tunnelling
through bone, singing

                    a small song.
"Ein Liedchen, Kinder!" The children ran away.
She moved about the yard like an old rag bird.
Still at war, she rose at dawn, watching out
for Rudi, come home on crutches,
the thin legs balancing his atom of life.

# Robert Schumann, Or: Musical Genius Begins with Affliction

It began with *A*—years before in a room
with a white piano and lyre-back chairs,
Schumann panted on a whore on a coverlet
and the oboe got its chance . . .

It never stops: .the alarm
going off in his head is a cry
in a thicket of its own making.
Cello Concerto in A minor,

Symphony in A, Phantasiestücke,
Concerto for Piano and Orchestra
in A minor, Opus 54: the notes
stack themselves onto the score-sheets

like unfamiliar furniture, the music
pulls higher and higher, and still
each phrase returns to *A*
no chord is safe from *A*

Years before, in a room with delicate chairs,
he was happy. There were no wretched sounds.
He was Adam naked in creation,
starting over as the sky rained apples.

# Happenstance

When you appeared it was as if
magnets cleared the air.
I had never seen that smile before
or your hair, flying silver. Someone
waving goodbye, she was silver, too.
Of course you didn't see me.
I called softly so you could choose
not to answer—then called again.
You turned in the light, your eyes
seeking your name.

# Small Town

Someone is sitting in the red house.
There is no way of telling who it is, although
the woman, indistinct, in the doorway must know;
and the man in the chestnut tree
who wields the binoculars
does not wish to be seen from the window.

The paint was put there by a previous owner.
The dog in the flower bed
is bound by indiscriminate love,
which is why he does not bark
and why in one of the darkened rooms
someone sits, a crackling vacuum.

The woman wears a pale blue nightgown
and stares vaguely upward. The man,
whose form appears clearly among the leaves,
is not looking at her
so much as she at him,
while away behind the town a farmer
weeps, plowing his fields by night
to avoid being laughed at during the day.

# The Snow King

In a far far land where men are men
And women are sun and sky,
The snow king paces. And light throws
A gold patina on the white spaces
Where sparrows lie frozen in hallways.

And he weeps for the sparrows, their clumped feathers:
Where is the summer that lasts forever,
The night as soft as antelope eyes?
The snow king roams the lime-filled spaces,
His cracked heart a slow fire, a garnet.

# Sightseeing

Come here, I want to show you something.
I inquired about the church yesterday:

the inner courtyard, also in ruin, has been left
exactly as the villagers found it

after the Allies left. What a consort
of broken dolls! Look, they were mounted

at the four corners of the third floor terrace
and the impact from the cobblestones

snapped off wings and other appendages.
The heads rolled the farthest. Someone

started to pile the limbs together—
from the weight of the pieces, an adult—

a deserter, perhaps, or a distraught priest.
Whoever it was, the job was interrupted,

so to speak, in mid-step: this forearm
could not have fallen so far from its owner

without assistance. The villagers,
come here to give thanks, took one look in

and locked the gates: "A terrible sign . . . "
But all this palaver about symbols and

"the ceremony of innocence drowned" is—
as you and I know—civilization's way

of manufacturing hope. Let's look
at the facts. Forget they are children of angels

and they become childish monsters.
Remember, and an arm gracefully upraised

is raised not in anger but a mockery of gesture.
The hand will hold both of mine. The vulgarity

of life in exemplary size is why
we've come to regard this abandoned

constellation, and why two drunks
would walk all the way crosstown

to look at a bunch of smashed statues.

# Upon Meeting Don L. Lee, In a Dream

He comes toward me with lashless eyes,
Always moving in the yellow half-shadows.
From his mouth I know he has never made love
To thin white boys in toilet stalls . . .

Among the trees, the black trees,
Women in robes stand, watching. They begin
To chant, stamping their feet in wooden cadences
As they stretch their beaded arms to him;

Moments slip by like worms.
"Seven years ago . . . " he begins; but
I cut him off: "Those years are gone—
What is there now?" He starts to cry; his eyeballs

Burst into flame. I can see caviar
Imbedded like buckshot between his teeth.
His hair falls out in clumps of burned-out wire.
The music grows like branches in the wind.

I lie down, chuckling as the grass curls around me.
He can only stand, fists clenched, and weep
Tears of iodine, while the singers float away,
Rustling on brown paper wings.

# "Teach Us to Number Our Days"

In the old neighborhood, each funeral parlor
is more elaborate than the last.
The alleys smell of cops, pistols bumping their thighs,
each chamber steeled with a slim blue bullet.

Low-rent balconies stacked to the sky.
A boy plays tic-tac-toe on a moon
crossed by TV antennae, dreams

he has swallowed a blue bean.
It takes root in his gut, sprouts
and twines upward, the vines curling
around the sockets and locking them shut.

And this sky, knotting like a dark tie?
The patroller, disinterested, holds all the beans.

August. The mums nod past, each a prickly heart on a sleeve.

# Nigger Song: An Odyssey

We six pile in, the engine churning ink:
We ride into the night.
Past factories, past graveyards
And the broken eyes of windows, we ride
Into the gray-green nigger night.

We sweep past excavation sites; the pits
Of gravel gleam like mounds of ice.
Weeds clutch at the wheels;
We laugh and swerve away, veering
Into the black entrails of the earth,
The green smoke sizzling on our tongues . . .

In the nigger night, thick with the smell of cabbages,
Nothing can catch us.
Laughter spills like gin from glasses,
And "yeah" we whisper, "yeah"
We croon, "yeah."

II

# Five Elephants

are walking towards me.
When morning is still a frozen
tear in the brain, they come
from the east, trunk to tail,
clumsy ballerinas.

How to tell them all evening
I refused consolation? Five umbrellas, five
willows, five bridges and their shadows!
They lift their trunks, hooking the sky
I would rush into, split

pod of quartz and lemon. I could say
they are five memories, but
that would be unfair.
Rather pebbles seeking refuge in the heart.
They move past me. I turn and follow,

and for hours we meet no one else.

# Geometry

I prove a theorem and the house expands:
the windows jerk free to hover near the ceiling,
the ceiling floats away with a sigh.

As the walls clear themselves of everything
but transparency, the scent of carnations
leaves with them. I am out in the open

and above the windows have hinged into butterflies,
sunlight glinting where they've intersected.
They are going to some point true and unproven.

# Champagne

The natives here have given up their backyards
and are happy living where we cannot see them,
No shade! The sky insists upon its blueness,
the baskets their roped ovals.
Gravel blinds us, blurring the road's shoulders.
Figures moving against the corduroyed hills
are not an industry to speak of, just
an alchemy whose yield is pleasure.

Come quickly—a whiff of yeast
means bubbles are forming, trapped
by sugar and air. The specialist who turns
30,000 bottles a day 10° to the right
lines up in a vaulted cellar
for an Italian red at the end of the day.
On either side for as far as we can see,
racks of unmarked bottles lying in cool fever.

Three centuries before in this dim corridor
a monk paused to sip, said it pricked
the tongue like stars. When we emerge
it is as difficult to remember the monk
as it is to see things as they are:
houses waver in the heat, stone walls
blaze. The hurt we feel is delicate—
all for ourselves and all for nothing.

# Night Watch

In this stucco house there is nothing but air.
The Mexican sky shivers toward morning.
I am on the four-star vacation from the wings
Of man to these halls draped in heavy matting
Where lizards hang from light fixtures.
From an invisible courtyard comes
The broken applause of castanets.

Romance may lurk in the land of white orchids,
But no slim-hipped Latin comes for me.
Coated servants scuttle through the halls.
I hear the morning wind around the house
As the light goes out
To the shanties in the mountains.

# The Secret Garden

I was ill, lying on my bed of old papers,
when you came with white rabbits in your arms;
and the doves scattered upwards, flying to mothers,
and the snails sighed under their baggage of stone . . .

Now your tongue grows like celery between us:
Because of our love-cries, cabbage darkens in its nest;
the cauliflower thinks of her pale, plump children
and turns greenish-white in a light like the ocean's.

I was sick, fainting in the smell of teabags,
when you came with tomatoes, a good poetry.
I am being wooed. I am being conquered
by a cliff of limestone that leaves chalk on my breasts.

# A Suite for Augustus

*1963*

That winter I stopped loving the President
And loved his dying. He smiled
From his frame on the chifferobe
And watched as I reined in each day
Using buttons for rosary beads.

Then tapwater rinsed orange through my underwear.
You moved away, and in tall white buildings
Typed speeches, each word-cluster a satellite,
A stone cherry that arced over the violent bay,
Broadcasting ball games and good will to Cuba . . .

But to me, stretched out under percale,
The cherry blinks sadly: Goodbye, goodbye,
Spinning into space. In this black place
I touch the doorknobs of my knees, begging to open
Me, an erector set, spilled and unpuzzled.

## D.C.

**1**

Roosters corn wooden dentures
pins & thimbles embroidery hoops
greenbacks & silver snuff & silver

brontosaurus bones couched on Smithsonian velvet

**2**

A bloodless finger pointing to heaven, you say,
is surely no more impossible than this city:
A no man's land, a capital askew,
a postcard framed by imported blossoms—
and now this outrageous cue stick
lying, reflected, on a black table.

**3**

Leaving his chair under the giant knee-cap,
he prowls the edge of the prune-black water.
Down the lane of clipped trees, a ghost trio
plays Dixie. His slaves have outlived him
in this life, too. Harmonicas breathe in,
the gray palms clap: "De broomstick's jumped, the world's
not wide."

*Planning the Perfect Evening*

I keep him waiting, tuck in the curtains,
buff my nails (such small pink eggshells).
As if for the last time, I descend the stair.

He stands penguin-stiff in a room
that's so quiet we forget it is there.
Now nothing, not even breath, can come

between us, not even the aroma of punch
and sneakers as we dance the length
of the gymnasium and crepe paper streams

down like cartoon lightning. Ah,
Augustus, where did you learn to samba?
And what is that lump below your cummerbund?

Stardust. The band folds up
resolutely, with plum-dark faces.
The night still chirps. Sixteen cars

caravan to Georgia for a terrace,
beer and tacos. Even this far south
a thin blue ice shackles the moon,

and I'm happy my glass sizzles with stars.
How far away the world! And how hulking
you are, my dear, my sweet black bear!

*Augustus Observes the Sunset*

July. The conspiracy of colors—
Ketchup, marshmallows, the tub of ice,
Bacon strips floating in pale soup.
The sun, like a dragon spreading its tail,
Burns the blue air to ribbons.

Eastward, the corn swelling in its sockets,
A wall of silence, growing.
What are you doing in your own backyard
Holding your coat in your arms?
There's so much left to do!—You pack.
Above spareribs and snow-puffed potatoes
The sky shakes like a flag.

*Wake*

Stranded in the middle of the nation like this,
I turn eastward, following rivers.
My heart, shy mulatto, wanders toward
The salt-edged contours of rock and sand
That stretch ahead into darkness:

But you stand in the way, a young boy
Appearing on the bank of the Potomac,
Profile turned to sudden metal
And your shirt-front luminous
Under a thicket of cherry boughs.

You open your mouth as if to say
*Tadpoles, pebbles,*
Each word a droplet of creme de menthe.
What reaches me is not your words
But your breath, exalted and spearmint.

*Back*

Three years too late, I'm scholarshipped
to Europe and back.
Four years, a language later, and
your 39th jet lands in Kuwait.
(Down

through columns of khaki and ribbons,
escorted at night by the radiance
of oil fields, you relax at last—
goat milk and scotch, no women, no
maple trees. You think: how far I've come)

This barnstorming that led no closer to you
has stuffed my knees into violets,
buried me in the emerald hearts of leaves.
They are like twenty-mark bills, soft
dollars, they bring me back.

III

# Belinda's Petition

(Boston, February, 1782)

To the honorable Senate and House
of Representatives of this Country,
new born: I am Belinda, an African,
since the age of twelve a Slave.
I will not take too much of your Time,
but to plead and place my pitiable Life
unto the Fathers of this Nation.

Lately your Countrymen have severed
the Binds of Tyranny. I would hope
you would consider the Same for me,
pure Air being the sole Advantage
of which I can boast in my present Condition.

As to the Accusation that I am Ignorant:
I received Existence on the Banks
of the Rio de Valta. All my Childhood
I expected nothing, if that be Ignorance.
The only Travelers were the Dead who returned
from the Ridge each Evening. How might
I have known of Men with Faces like the Moon,
who would ride toward me steadily for twelve Years?

# The House Slave

The first horn lifts its arm over the dew-lit grass
and in the slave quarters there is a rustling—
children are bundled into aprons, cornbread

and water gourds grabbed, a salt pork breakfast taken.
I watch them driven into the vague before-dawn
while their mistress sleeps like an ivory toothpick

and Massa dreams of asses, rum and slave-funk.
I cannot fall asleep again. At the second horn,
the whip curls across the backs of the laggards—

sometimes my sister's voice, unmistaken, among them.
"Oh! pray," she cries. "Oh! pray!" Those days
I lie on my cot, shivering in the early heat,

and as the fields unfold to whiteness,
and they spill like bees among the fat flowers,
I weep. It is not yet daylight.

# David Walker (1785-1830)

Free to travel, he still couldn't be shown how lucky
he was: *They strip and beat and drag us about*
*like rattlesnakes.* Home on Brattle Street, he took in the sign
on the door of the slop shop. All day at the counter—
white caps, ale-stained pea coats. Compass needles,
eloquent as tuning forks, shivered, pointing north.
Evenings, the ceiling fan sputtered like a second pulse.
*Oh Heaven! I am full!! I can hardly move my pen!!!*

On the faith of an eye-wink, pamphlets were stuffed
into trouser pockets. Pamphlets transported
in the coat linings of itinerant seamen, jackets
ringwormed with salt traded drunkenly to pursers
in the Carolinas, pamphlets ripped out, read aloud:
*Men of colour, who are also of sense.*
Outrage. Incredulity. Uproar in state legislatures.

*We are the most wretched, degraded and abject set*
*of beings that ever lived since the world began.*
The jewelled canaries in the lecture halls tittered,
pressed his dark hand between their gloves.
Every half-step was no step at all.
Every morning, the man on the corner strung a fresh
bunch of boots from his shoulders. "I'm happy!" he said.
"I never want to live any better or happier than
when I can get a-plenty of boots and shoes to clean!"

A second edition. A third.
The abolitionist press is *perfectly appalled.*
*Humanity, kindness and the fear of the Lord*
*does not consist in protecting devils.* A month—
his person (is that all?) found face-down
in the doorway at Brattle Street,
his frame slighter than friends remembered.

# The Abduction

The bells, the cannons, the houses black with crepe,
all for the great Harrison! The citizenry of Washington
clotted the avenue—I among them, Solomon Northrup
from Saratoga Springs, free papers in my pocket, violin
under arm, my new friends Brown and Hamilton by my side.

Why should I have doubted them? The wages were good.
While Brown's tall hat collected pennies at the tent flap,
Hamilton's feet did a jig on a tightrope,
pigs squealed invisibly from the bleachers and I fiddled.

I remember how the windows rattled with each report.
Then the wine, like a pink lake, tipped.
I was lifted—the sky swivelled, clicked into place.

I floated on water I could not drink. Though the pillow
was stone, I climbed no ladders in that sleep.

I woke and found myself alone, in darkness and in chains.

# The Transport of Slaves
# From Maryland to Mississippi

(On August 22, 1839, a wagonload of slaves broke their chains,
killed two white men, and would have escaped, had not a slave
woman helped the Negro driver mount his horse and ride for
help.)

*I don't know if I helped him up*
*because I thought he was our salvation*
*or not.* Left for dead in the middle
of the road, dust hovering around the body
like a screen of mosquitoes
shimmering in the hushed light.
*The skin across his cheekbones*
*burst open like baked yams—*
deliberate, the eyelids came apart—
*his eyes were my eyes in a yellower face.*
*Death and salvation—*one accommodates the other.
*I am no brute. I got feelings.*
*He might have been a son of mine.*

                        *


"The Negro Gordon, barely escaping with his life, rode
into the plantation just as his pursuers came into sight.
The neighborhood was rallied and a search begun.
Some of the Negroes had taken to the woods but
were routed, ending this most shocking affray and murder."

                        *


Eight miles south of Portsmouth, the last handcuff

broke clean from the skin. The last thing
the driver saw were the trees, improbable as broccoli,
before he was clubbed from behind. Sixty slaves
poured off the wagon, smelly, half-numb, free.

Baggage man Petit rushed in with his whip.
*Some nigger's laid on another one's leg*, he thought
before he saw they were loose. *Hold it!* he yelled;
but not even the wenches stopped. To his right
Atkins dropped under a crown of clubs. They didn't
even flinch. *Wait. You ain't supposed to act this way.*

# Pamela

" . . . the hour was come when the man must act, or forever be a slave."

At two, the barnyard settled
into fierce silence—anvil,
water pump glinted
as though everything waited
for the first step.
She stepped
into the open. The wind
lifted—behind her,
fields spread their sails.

*There really is a star up there and moss on the trees.* She discovered if she kept a steady pace, she could walk forever. The idea pleased her, and she hummed a hymn to herself— Peach Point, Silk Hope, Beaver Bend. It seemed that the further north she went, the freer she became. The stars were plates for good meat; if she reached, they flashed and became coins.

White quiet. Night pushed over the hill.
The woods hiss with cockleburs,
each a small woolly head.
She feels old, older
than these friendly shadows
who, like the squirrels, don't come too near.
Knee-deep in muscadine, she watches them coming,
snapping the brush. They are
smiling, rifles crossed on their chests.

# Someone's Blood

I stood at 6 a.m. on the wharf,
thinking: *This is Independence, Missouri.*
*I am to stay here. The boat goes on to New Orleans.*
My life seemed minutes old, and here it was ending.

I was silent, although she clasped me
and asked forgiveness for giving me life.
As the sun broke the water into a thousand needles
tipped with the blood from someone's finger,

the boat came gently apart from the wharf.
I watched till her face could not distinguish itself
from that shadow floated on broken sunlight.
I stood there. I could not help her. I forgive.

# Cholera

At the outset, hysteria.
Destruction, the conjurers intoned.
Some dragged themselves off at night
to die in the swamp, to lie down
with the voices of mud and silk.

>           *I know moonrise, I know starrise*

Against orders
the well and almost-well were assembled
and marched into the wood. When
a dry open place was found, halted.
The very weak got a piece of board
and fires were built, though the evening was warm,
Said the doctor, You'll live.

>           *I walk in de moonlight, I walk in de*
>               *starlight*

Who could say but that it wasn't anger
had to come out somehow? Pocketed filth.
The pouring-away of pints of pale fluid.

>           *I'll walk in de graveyard, I'll walk*
>               *through de graveyard*

Movement, dark and silken.
The dry-skinned conjurers circling the fire.
Here is pain, they whispered, And it is all ours.
Who would want to resist them?
By camplight their faces had taken on

the frail finality of ash.

> *I'll lie in de grave and stretch out my*
> *arms*

Well,
that was too much for the doctor.
Strip 'em! he ordered. And they
were slicked down with bacon fat and
superstition strapped from them
to the beat of the tam-tam. Those strong enough
rose up too, and wailed as they leapt.
It was a dance of unusual ferocity.

# The Slave's Critique of Practical Reason

Ain't got a reason
to run away—
leastways, not one
would save my life.
So I scoop speculation
into a hopsack.
I scoop fluff till
the ground rears white
and I'm the only dark
spot in the sky.

All day the children
sit in the weeds
to wait out the heat
with the rattlers.
All day Our Lady
of the Milk-Tooth
attends them
while I, the Owl
of the Broken Spirit
keep dipping and
thinking up tunes
that fly off quick
as they hit
the air. As far
as I can see,

it's hotter in heaven
than in the cool
cool earth. I know
'cause I've been there,
a stony mote
circling the mindless
blue, dropping rows
of little clouds,
no-good reasons
for sale.

# Kentucky, 1833

It is Sunday, day of roughhousing. We are let out in the
woods. The young boys wrestle and butt their heads together
like sheep—a circle forms; claps and shouts fill the air.
The women, brown and glossy, gather round the banjo player,
or simply lie in the sun, legs and aprons folded. The weather's
an odd monkey—any other day he's on our backs, his cotton eye
everywhere; today the light sifts down like the finest cornmeal,
coating our hands and arms with a dust. God's dust, old woman
Acker says. She's the only one who could read to us from the
Bible, before Massa forbade it. On Sundays, something hangs
in the air, a hallelujah, a skitter of brass, but we can't
call it by name and it disappears.

Then Massa and his gentlemen friends come to bet on the boys.
They guffaw and shout, taking sides, red-faced on the edge of
the boxing ring. There is more kicking, butting, and scuffling—
the winner gets a dram of whiskey if he can drink it all in
one swig without choking.

Jason is bucking and prancing about—Massa said his name
reminded him of some sailor, a hero who crossed an ocean,
looking for a golden cotton field. Jason thinks he's been
born to great things—a suit with gold threads, vest and all.
Now the winner is sprawled out under a tree and the sun, that
weary tambourine, hesitates at the rim of the sky's green light.
It's a crazy feeling that carries through the night; as if the
sky were an omen we could not understand, the book that, if we
could read, would change our lives.

IV

# Adolescence—I

In water-heavy nights behind grandmother's porch
We knelt in the tickling grasses and whispered:
Linda's face hung before us, pale as a pecan,
And it grew wise as she said:
    "A boy's lips are soft,
    As soft as baby's skin."
The air closed over her words.
A firefly whirred near my ear, and in the distance
I could hear streetlamps ping
Into miniature suns
Against a feathery sky.

# Adolescence—II

Although it is night, I sit in the bathroom, waiting.
Sweat prickles behind my knees, the baby-breasts are alert.
Venetian blinds slice up the moon; the tiles quiver in pale strips.

Then they come, the three seal men with eyes as round
As dinner plates and eyelashes like sharpened tines.
They bring the scent of licorice. One sits in the washbowl,

One on the bathtub edge; one leans against the door.
"Can you feel it yet?" they whisper.
I don't know what to say, again. They chuckle,

Patting their sleek bodies with their hands.
"Well, maybe next time." And they rise,
Glittering like pools of ink under moonlight,

And vanish. I clutch at the ragged holes
They leave behind, here at the edge of darkness.
Night rests like a ball of fur on my tongue.

# Adolescence—III

With Dad gone, Mom and I worked
The dusky rows of tomatoes.
As they glowed orange in sunlight
And rotted in shadow, I too
Grew orange and softer, swelling out
Starched cotton slips.

The texture of twilight made me think of
Lengths of Dotted Swiss. In my room
I wrapped scarred knees in dresses
That once went to big-band dances;
I baptized my earlobes with rosewater.
Along the window-sill, the lipstick stubs
Glittered in their steel shells.

Looking out at the rows of clay
And chicken manure, I dreamed how it would happen:
He would meet me by the blue spruce,
A carnation over his heart, saying,
"I have come for you, Madam;
I have loved you in my dreams."
At his touch, the scabs would fall away.
Over his shoulder, I see my father coming toward us:
He carries his tears in a bowl,
And blood hangs in the pine-soaked air.

# The Boast

At the dinner table, before the baked eggplant,
you tell the story of your friend, Ira,
how he kept a three-foot piranha in his basement.
"It was this long," you say, extending your arms,
"And it was striped, with silver scales and blue shadows."

The man with purple eyes lifts his eyebrows;
you laugh at his joke about the lady
in the sausage suit, your toes find his
under the table, and he is yours.

Evening expires in a yawn of stars.
But on the walk home,
when he pulls you into the hedges,
and the black tongues of leaves flutter,
and those boogy-man eyes glitter,
there won't be time for coming back
with lies, with lies.

# The Kadava Kumbis Devise a Way to Marry for Love

I will marry this clump of flowers
and throw it into the well!

There is no comfort in poverty.
"Better," they say, "to give yourself

to the soil under your feet
than to a man without jewels.

Who can feast off wind?"
So bring the gongs and the

old women—let us mourn
the loss of my youthful husband!

Where his frail hands paused
breath lingered, so that I am now

restless, a perfumed fan.
Who has suffered once

is not subject to pride.
I will marry again—perhaps to

that ragged man on the hill,
watching from a respectful distance.

# Spy

She walked alone, as she did every morning.
Hers the narrow sidewalk, the corroded lamppost.
Larks thrilled the apricot air. Barbed crucifixes

Against the sky, the haloes of mist around streetlamps—
They reminded her of Jesus on a gilded altar
And Mama in a blue apron, praying.

Where were the oily midnights of depravity?
A woman of hard edges, blonde with dark armpits—
Where was she but always coming in from the cold?

# First Kiss

And it was almost a boy who undid
the double sadness I'd sealed away.
He built a house in a meadow
no one stopped to admire,

and wore wrong clothes. Nothing
seemed to get in his way.
I promised him anything
if he would go. He smiled

and left. How
to re-create his motives,
irretrievable

as a gasp? Where else
to find him, counter-rising
in me, almost a boy. . . .

# Then Came Flowers

I should have known if you gave me flowers
They would be chrysanthemums.
The white spikes singed my fingers.
I cried out; they spilled from the green tissue
And spread at my feet in a pool of soft fire.

If I begged you to stay, what good would it do me?
In the bed, you would lay the flowers between us.
I will pick them up later, arrange them with pincers.
All night from the bureau they'll watch me, their
Plumage as proud, as cocky as firecrackers.

# Pearls

You have broken the path of the dragonfly
who visits my patio at the hour when
the sky has nearly forgotten the sun.
You have come to tell me
how happy we are, but I know
what you would and would not do
to make us happy. For example this necklace
before me: white eyes,
a noose of guileless tears.

# Nexus

I wrote stubbornly into the evening.
At the window, a giant praying mantis
rubbed his monkey wrench head against the glass,
begging vacantly with pale eyes;

and the commas leapt at me like worms
or miniature scythes blackened with age.
The praying mantis screeched louder,
his ragged jaws opening onto formlessness.

I walked outside;
the grass hissed at my heels.
Up ahead in the lapping darkness
he wobbled, magnified and absurdly green,
a brontosaurus, a poet.

V

# Notes from a Tunisian Journal

This nutmeg stick of a boy in loose trousers!
Little coffee pots in the coals, a mint on the tongue.

The camels stand in all their vague beauty—
at night they fold up like pale accordions.

All the hedges are singing with yellow birds!
A boy runs by with lemons in his hands.

Food's perfume, breath is nourishment.
The stars crumble, salt above eucalyptus fields.

# The Sahara Bus Trip

---

## I. *Departure*

Roofless houses, cartons of chalk,
catch the sky in their mirrors of air.
Intake of breath. Crisp
trees hung with sour oranges.
Hunched in the unnatural light, you wait
for the driver to start this bus forward.
Dust scatters in the pus-filled eyes
of children running after us, waving.
How small they are! They are getting smaller.

## II. *The Discovery of Oranges*

*At night they quiver imperceptibly until*
*the leaves rustle; their perforated skins*
*give off a faint heat.*
Only the Arab knows the heart of the orange:
*she tears herself apart to give us relief.*
We spend 200 milliemes for a bag of oranges
so sweet our tongues lie dreaming in the juice.

## III. *The Salt Sea*

If, at the end of the Atlantic,
Columbus had found only an absence of water,
this English tourist would have been there
to capture that void with a wide-angle lens.
Here, the wind blows from nowhere to nowhere
across a plain transformed by salt
into a vision of light. One bug,
black and white, dusted with salt, crawls
among orange peels that flare up like

brittle flowers. *You could not live here,*
he says. *It is not so astonishing,*
*close your mouths.*

IV. *The Discovery of Sandroses*

Each inconsolable thought sprouts
a tear of salt which blossoms,
sharpens into a razored petal.
Now we have a bouquet of stone roses.
The bedouins are hawking the new miracle,
600 milliemes, a few francs!
You buy me a large one.
By the roadside, the boys pose with foxes—
those diseased bastard eyes, those crumbling smiles.

V. *Hotel Nefta*

We disembark, the bus wheezing
like a punctured furnace.
The Englishman has set his tripod up
and is shooting the green interference of palms.
It is tricky light. Tomorrow the trip back,
our fingers exhaling small, tangy breaths.
What a light-hearted whistle you have!
It reminds me of water—so far-away,
so clear, it must come from the sky.

# For Kazuko

The bolero, silk-tassled, the fuchsia
scarf come off: all that black hair

for the asking! You are unbraiding
small braids, your face full

behind a curtain of dark breath. Why
am I surprised when your lids emerge

from the fragrant paint? Now the couch
is baring its red throat, and now

you must understand me: your breasts,
so tiny, wound—or more precisely, echo

all the breasts which cannot swell, which
we prefer. I would like to lose myself

in those hushing thighs; but
sadness is not enough. A phallus

walks your dreams, Kazuko, lovely and
unidentified. Here is an anthology of wishes:

if fucking were graceful, desire an alibi.

# Beauty and the Beast

Darling, the plates have been cleared away,
the servants are in their quarters.
What lies will we lie down with tonight?
The rabbit pounding in your heart, my

child legs, pale from a life of petticoats?
My father would not have had it otherwise
when he trudged the road home with our souvenirs.
You are so handsome it eats my heart away . . .

Beast, when you lay stupid with grief
at my feet, I was too young to see anything
die. Outside, the roses are folding
lip upon red lip. I miss my sisters—

they are standing before their clouded mirrors.
Gray animals are circling under the windows.
Sisters, don't you see what will snatch you up—
the expected, the handsome, the one who needs us?

# His Shirt

does not show his
true colors. Ice-

blue and of stuff
so common

anyone
could have bought it,

his shirt
is known only

to me, and only
at certain times

of the day.
At dawn

it is a flag
in the middle

of a square
waiting to catch

chill light.
Unbuttoned, it's

a sail surprised
by boundless joy.

In candlelight at turns
a penitent's

scarf or beggar's
fleece, his shirt is

inapproachable.
It is the very shape

and tint
of desire

and could be mistaken
for something quite

fragile and
ordinary.

# Great Uncle Beefheart

It was not as if he didn't try
to tell us: first he claimed
the velvet armchair, then the sun
on the carpet before it. Silence,
too, he claimed, although
we tried to spoil it with humming
and children's games. There was
that much charm left in the world.

It was not as if he didn't want
to believe us: he kept himself
neat. Behind his head, the anti-
macassar darkened, surrendered
the fragrance of bergamot.
Things creaked when he touched
them, so he stopped that, too.
He called us "dear little bugs,"

and it was not as if he
*acted* strange, though our mother
told her mother once
at least his heart was bigger
than any other man's.
That's when we called him
Great Uncle Beefheart; and it was not
as if he listened: he just

walked outdoors. Sunflowers,
wildly prosperous, took

the daylight and shook it
until our vision ran.
We found him in his shirtsleeves
in the onion patch, shivering
as he cried *I can't go back in
there, I ain't wearing no clothes.*

# The Son

All the toothy Fräuleins are left behind:
blood machinery pumps the distance between you.
At the moment the landing gear
groans into the belly,
Mama's outside the window
in her shawl and her seed pearls.
She comes for help—your brother's
knocked down while restraining an inmate
and the family's counting on you . . .

A year ago Wagner sang you down the Rhine.
You stood in the failing light, certain
the Lorelei would toss you her comb.
Life could not bank and drop
you on the coal shores of Pittsburgh,
the house by factory light opening
its reluctant arms to boarders.

# Corduroy Road

We strike camp on that portion of road completed
during the day. The strip of sky above me
darkens: this afternoon when it lurched into view
I felt air swoop down, and breathed it in.

*Instruction:*
*Avoiding bogs and unduly rough terrain*
*Clear a track two rods wide*
*From Prairie du Chien to Fort Howard at Green Bay.*

Today Carlton devised an interesting pastime.
From each trunk the axe has razed
a startled, upturned face awaits
refinement by the penknife:
The Jester. The Statesman. The Sot. The Maiden.

*The symbol of motion is static, finite,*
*And kills by the coachload. Chances of perishing*
*On the road are ten to one, calculated*
*According to the following table of casualties:*
*1. By horses running away.*
*2. By overturning.*
*3. By drowning.*
*4. By murder.*
*5. By explosion.*

Whenever a tree is felled, I think of a thousand blankets
ripped into sparks, or that the stillness itself
has been found and torn open with bare hands.
What prevails a man to hazard his person in the Wisconsin Forests
is closer to contrition than anything: the wild honey
blazing from outstretched palms, a skunk bagged and eaten in tears.

# Ö

Shape the lips to an *o*, say *a*.
That's *island*.

One word of Swedish has changed the whole neighborhood.
When I look up, the yellow house on the corner
is a galleon stranded in flowers. Around it

the wind. Even the high roar of a leaf-mulcher
could be the horn-blast from a ship
as it skirts the misted shoals.

We don't need much more to keep things going.
Families complete themselves
and refuse to budge from the present,
the present extends its glass forehead to sea
(backyard breezes, scattered cardinals)

and if, one evening, the house on the corner
took off over the marshland,
neither I nor my neighbor
would be amazed. Sometimes

a word is found so right it trembles
at the slightest explanation.
You start out with one thing, end
up with another, and nothing's
like it used to be, not even the future.